CALM

ANXIOUS DOG

How To Stop Your Dog Anxiety

And Regain Serenity

Table of Content

Introduction 1
Chapter One 4
Understand Your Dog Behavior 4
Chapter Two 12
Understanding Dog Anxiety 12
Chapter Three 24
Secrets To Reduce Dog Anxiety 24
Chapter Four 27
Five Things You Should Know About Dog Anxiety 27
Chapter Five 31
Effects Of Anxiety On The Health And Life Expectancy Of Your Dog 31
Chapter Six 34
Types Of Dog Anxiety 34
Chapter Seven 40
Dealing With Dog Separation Anxiety 40
Chapter Eight 61
Dealing With Social Anxiety 61
Chapter Nine 79

Dealing With Dog Noise Anxiety 79
Chapter Ten.. 104
Anti-Anxiety Drugs And Dogs 104
Chapter Eleven.. 120
Natural Remedies For Anxious Dogs................. 120
Chapter Twelve 129
Ten Relaxing Tips For Anxious Dogs................ 129
Chapter Thirteen 140
Extra Ways To Keep Your Dog Happy And Healthy 140
Conclusion 144
Author Note 147

© **Copyright 2020 by Josh Roswell**

All rights reserved.

This document is geared towards providing exact and reliable information in regards to the topic and issue covered. The publication is sold with the idea that the publisher is not required to render accounting, officially permitted, or otherwise, qualified services. If advice is necessary, legal or professional, a practiced individual in the profession should be ordered.

- From a Declaration of Principles which was accepted and approved equally by a Committee of the American Bar Association and a Committee of Publishers and Associations.

In no way is it legal to reproduce, duplicate, or transmit any part of this document in either electronic means or in printed format. Recording of this publication is strictly prohibited and any storage of this document is not allowed unless with written permission from the publisher. All rights reserved.

The information provided herein is stated to be truthful and consistent, in that any liability, in terms of inattention or otherwise, by any usage or abuse of any policies, processes, or directions contained within is the solitary and utter responsibility of the recipient reader. Under no circumstances will any legal responsibility or blame be held against the publisher for any reparation, damages, or monetary loss due to the information herein, either directly or indirectly.

Respective authors own all copyrights not held by the publisher. The information herein is offered for informational purposes solely, and is universal as so. The presentation of the information is without contract or any type of guarantee assurance.

The trademarks that are used are without any consent, and the publication of the trademark is without permission or backing by the trademark owner. All trademarks and brands within this book are for clarifying purposes only and are the owned by the owners themselves, not affiliated with this document.

Disclaimer

The Author is providing this book and its contents on an "as is" basis and make no warranties of any kind with respect to this book or its contents. The author assume no responsibility for errors, inaccuracies, omissions, or any other inconsistencies herein. The content of this book is for informational purposes only and is not intended to diagnose, treat, cure, or prevent any condition or disease. The publisher and the author make no guarantees concerning the level of success you may experience by following the advice and strategies contained in this book, and you accept the risk that results will differ for each individual.

INTRODUCTION

There is no shortage of reasons why dogs are wonderful companions. They are loyal, offer unconditional love, bring joy every day and never respond. These are all fantastic qualities for any creature that claims to be man's best friend. Dogs were one of the closest pets to men who live with them and, in most cases, they join in such a way that they represent another family member, so their behavior directly affects the common welfare. Changes in dog behavior represent a serious problem that threatens not only the physical integrity and general well-being of the dog but also that of the people around it. In this way, studies that focus on solving animal behavior problems are indirectly helping to improve the quality of life of the family and even that of the community; in the same way, they reduce the risk of domestic exclusion of the animal, since most of the dog's behavioral problems generally lead to the sacrifice or abandonment of the dog.

All these situations often cause anxiety problems in humans. Dogs also get anxious, and as people, anxiety in dogs can be the result of a number of triggers. Dogs may be anxious for a wide range of things, it could be something innocent like the phone ringing that makes their dogs bark anxiously, or it could be the sound of you picking up the car keys to get out. Your dog walks immediately across the floor. Therefore, since anything could trigger an anxiety reaction, it is important to realize that it is not what they do that matters, but the way you react that will help them most. Dog anxiety affects many of our dogs, be it fear of loud noises such as fireworks or thunderstorms, or the stress that is triggered by leaving them alone. The result of this anxiety is manifested in what often seems a case of dog misbehavior, which can lead to an incorrect approach to solving the problem. Take, for example, a dog that poops around the house. It may seem to the owner that he needs more training at home instead of worrying about being anxious.

Similarly, a dog that chews everything if left alone can be labeled as a destructive dog instead of an anxious dog.

What you should remember is that your dog is not intentionally bad, just scared or nervous and it is up to you like your dog father to try to take care of him. Prevention is the best thing you can do, but in unexpected situations, understanding your dog anxiety will go a long way.

CHAPTER ONE
UNDERSTAND YOUR DOG BEHAVIOR

Understanding your dog behavior can make a difference! The dog's behavior and how to understand it has always been a challenge. Even if we are dealing with a different species and one with which we cannot communicate in human terms; through the different scientific investigations over the years, we now have a basic understanding of how dogs work. Our first contact with the descriptions and concepts of dog behavior dates back to the late 1800s when JHWalsh made the first attempt to describe the different breeds and their temperament in 1874. Sadly, since they were all recorded by the same man and because at that time, there was not much research nor materials available in dogs; almost all descriptions of temperament and behavior (even today) seem very similar to each other.

Genetically inherited behavior

There has been much debate about how much of a dog's behavior is actually inherited and has some resemblance to that of wolves, wild dogs, etc.

The environmental impact on the behavior of a dog

Every creature on earth has been shaped by the environment in which it lives. For instance, if you have a litter of puppies and let them grow in the same environment without any human interference, they will grow up behaving quite similar to each other. On the other hand, if you breed these puppies in different homes with different dog owners, you will have a variety of canine behaviors, from a playful or hyperactive dog to an anxious or scary dog.

Trained (Classic) dog behaviors

Although a lot of people think that dog training is restricted to obedience, protection, sports, etc. The truth is that we train our dogs daily by encouraging or discouraging behaviors. For example, jumping on visitors; Personally, I can only name a handful of dog owners who have dealt with this problem from the beginning, not allowing this habit to become a model of dog behavior in the first place. Too many people do not face the behavior when it starts and then feels overwhelmed when their dog is an adult. There are so many behaviors that we instill in our dogs daily without even knowing it.

How different we are from each other

First, dogs are completely different from us, and although this is obvious, due to lack of knowledge, we tend to handle them in a way that they don't understand, in our human way. Your brain, eyes, nose, sense of touch are different from humans. For instance, the part of the human brain that refers to our sense of smell is only a few grams in weight, but in a dog's brain, the part that is its center of smell occupies one-seventh of the total volume of the brain.

We can hear about 20,000 acoustic vibrations; Dogs can hear (depending on the breed and the individual dog) anywhere between 40,000 and 100,000 acoustic vibrations (on average 40,000-65,000). This is one of the reasons why the dog acts when it turns on certain machines or devices. These machines can produce penetrating noises that go beyond our hearing abilities, but that influence the behavior of our dog.

We also see the world around us in totally different ways. Our eyes and those of our dog are not the same:

- Humans have the ability to see colors, we are capable of spatial vision and we can judge the distances between us and objects, we can see and recognize a motionless object. However, we have limitations to recognize moving objects at a greater distance.

- Dogs do not see colors in the way we see them, still objects both in the immediate vicinity and in the distance are not recognizable to them (they see them only as shapes and shadows), on the other hand, they see objects, both close and at a greater distance, they can see with great precision and can recognize their owners, for example, at a greater distance than humans can only rely on their individual and characteristic movements.

And if we had to compare emotions, for example:

- Humans have a few thousand "recognized" and named emotions that come from some different emotional groups that we use in our daily lives.

- Dogs have some basic emotions, mainly related to basic actions that help them survive in nature. Many of them are the product of fear or are driven by their instincts as prey; In addition, there are some of the positive emotions that they share between the members of the pack and the littermates or in some rituals that help them reconnect and survive as a pack.

Now you are probably wondering why this is important. To understand dog and dog behavior patterns, you must understand the fact that you are dealing with different species and that dogs do not see or understand the world around us.

They have no emotional abilities, since many dog owners often consider them "vengeful," etc. For instance, when a dog does something that seems to take revenge on his guide, or when we expect our dog to follow a simple logical sequence of training for a given action. Dogs simply cannot do those things if we understand this basic difference; We have the opportunity to approach our dog in a different way, which will save us time and patience.

To highlight the significance of understanding dog behavior, I will mention that, according to researchers, the main reason why dogs end up in dog shelters is due to dog behavior problems. Studies on this were conducted in 2000 and the results show that more than 40% of dogs ended up in dog shelters and dog rescues due to behavioral problems, today this number is even greater, and some researchers say this trend will continue.

You must understand the dog's behavior to avoid dog behavior problems; You must understand how the environment influences your dog's behavior in everyday life and also how to deal with it. Most of us drive cars and yet, a lot of us have no idea what to do when our car breaks down and what happened to cause it. Most people don't know anything about the engine or how to properly maintain it or distinguish those strange sounds that warn us that something is wrong, so we hope helplessly that strange sound becomes an engine failure.

The dog's behavior is somewhat similar. It is who the dog really is and not knowing how to read it will lead to dog behavior problems, which in many cases are identified and addressed only when they become unmanageable.

CHAPTER TWO
UNDERSTANDING DOG ANXIETY

Fear, anxiety, phobia. No matter what you call it, it is distressing when your beloved dog complains, screams or tries to hide behind the couch to escape a storm, emptiness or Independence Day fireworks. No matter the cause, it is difficult to assure your dog that everything is fine when he sees that his world is running out. Although fear, anxiety, and phobias are not all the same, they all have to do with your dog's need for safety. Fear is a response to a perceived threat. The autonomic nervous system of a dog responds to the sensed threat by triggering a response throughout the body. Anxiety is the anticipation of a terrifying event based on past experiences. A phobia is simply an irrational fear that leads to anxiety and frightening symptoms.

The three types of dog anxiety can be managed by an attentive owner. It is important to understand your limitations when working with your dog and seek help from your dog's veterinarian or an animal behavior expert if fear and anxiety make your dog aggressive. Most times, dog anxiety disorders can be managed by pet owners if they have a basic understanding of how anxiety, phobias, and fears work in dogs, how they are and how to tell the dog that everything will be fine.

Many people experience stress and anxiety at various levels throughout their lives, due to problems at work or in social life. While most can find ways to control stress levels, others may find that the pressure they suffer is extremely harmful to their mental and physical health. The same goes for dogs, which is due to their lack of ability to rationalize problems, can quickly begin to show signs of poor health due to emotional distress. There are numerous reasons why a dog may begin to feel anxious, mainly due to his social life and daily routine.

While these causes may seem minor to an outside observer, stress and anxiety can cause a dog to experience behavioral changes (such as increased lethargy or even aggression) and may even be a factor behind the development of health problems (such as insomnia, stomach ulcers, hair loss, weight loss, and compromised immune system). Therefore, it is advisable to neutralize the causes of anxiety in a dog's life before they become a serious problem.

Like humans, dogs experience anxiety. While it is unpleasant, it is a normal and even healthy emotion. Dog anxiety can affect all breeds, but it can affect each dog differently. Although this is something that all dogs experience from time to time, if disproportionate levels of anxiety are not controlled, a dog can develop an anxiety disorder. If left untreated, the dog's anxiety can lead to behavioral and other problems.

Canine anxiety symptoms

The dog's anxiety symptoms are easy to detect once you understand how dogs communicate their feelings. Despite what we might expect, dogs don't really talk to us. However, they communicate volumes with their body language and actions; they even inform us about anxiety. The symptoms of dog anxiety include:

- Sounds: Dogs can moan, groan, complain, bark excessively or howl when they are anxious or scared. These sounds may differ from your normal sounds. The moan of a dog by surprise or a bark of happiness upon hearing him enter through the door may seem different from a noise produced by fear. Owners know when their dogs respond abnormally to stimuli. The more time you get to spend with your dog, the easier it will be to detect reactions based on fear.

- Stimulation: dogs that are scary can give way to the house and cannot settle in their favorite places. They could lie down for a few minutes and then jump to find a new place. Sometimes they act like they are looking for something, maybe a place where they feel safe.

- Destruction: Some pet owners blame boredom for the destructive tendencies of their dogs, oblivious to the fact that even anxious and fearful dogs become destructive dogs. The dog begins to chew, dig or scratch doors and other objects in an attempt to escape what they fear. The anxiety centers of the brain trigger the fight or flight response, and the destruction resulting from fear is usually an attempt to escape what triggered their fear reaction.

- Shaking: fear makes dogs shake or shake. You can feel it when you place your hands on your dog's side or see waves that move along your dog's hips. Crouching often accompanies agitation.

- Drooling: Drooling and panting are also part of the fear response. Excessive salivation is another reaction of the autonomic nervous system when combat or flight instincts are activated in dogs.

- Trivial mistakes: scared dogs often forget their training to go to the bathroom and carpets, rugs or other prohibited areas.

- Yawning: It may seem strange that yawning in excess is a symptom of dog anxiety, but the same internal mechanism that triggers all other reactions can also make your dog yawn.

Dog anxiety symptoms can often be confused with other problems. An anxious dog that walks around the house, groans and dirties the carpet can be reproached for being a "bad dog" when he is simply afraid of something or anxious. It is also important to rule out other causes, such as a stomachache.

What are the causes of anxiety in dogs?

There are many factors that can cause anxiety in dogs, which include:

Introducing a new family member

This is important because, although dogs generally enjoy company, they sometimes initially care about new family members. To successfully introduce a new pet or child to your home, do it slowly and make your dog easier to change. Especially for dogs with only one child, this is a great chance that he is not used to, which can cause anxiety and stress.

Visitors

Whether it's a weekend trip for girls, a surfer's cousin or an extended mother-in-law stay, visitors can make any puppy feel anxious. Even if your dog is generally doing well under pressure, anyone new to your environment can cause concern.

If you are going to receive visitors, make sure your dog has enough space for himself if he is afraid or anxious. Try to follow your routine, if possible, including walks and regular meals.

Owner separation

Separation anxiety in dogs is very common, especially of dogs that have been in a shelter or have experienced abandonment in their previous lives or of dog breeds, particularly prone to separation anxiety. This anxiety can be triggered by a long and short duration of being left alone, depending on the dog.

Moving houses or changing rooms

Moving can be stressful for just anyone, even dogs! The idea of filling your entire environment and living in a completely different place can cause anxiety to even the calmest puppies. In addition to moving, important changes in environments, such as moving furniture or remodeling, can also cause canine anxiety.

Past experiences

The reality is that some dogs, especially those adopted by a shelter or found as stray dogs, have faced difficult times and dramatic experiences.

Sometimes, these traumas manifest themselves in everyday things that would not normally be a reason for concern. If you notice that your dog reacts poorly to normally harmless things, it may show anxiety about past experiences.

An underlying disease

Dogs may show signs of anxiety and stress if they experience another disease or illness. It is important to keep in mind that untreated anxiety can lead to depression in dogs. If the above anxiety symptoms are related to other health problems that you may notice, check with your veterinarian to make sure that something more serious is not happening. These are just some of the reasons why a dog may feel anxious and the causes of canine anxiety will depend on the dog's breed and its typical behavior.

Why do some dogs have anxiety and others don't?

Dogs are like people. Genetics, background, life experiences, health, nutrition, and current events all work collectively to determine how they feel. In some canines, these forces blend to create a dog that will develop an anxiety disorder. In others, the same situation can lead to momentary fear, followed by curiosity. As with any other family member or friend, you should know your dog and understand his personality to prevent and deal with individual oddities. When you buy a dog, you are committed to the well-being of the dog for life. As a responsible owner of a dog, you should spend time with your dog and do everything possible to meet your needs and create a safe environment. When you can read your dog's body language, you can avoid situations that produce excessive anxiety. You can also create an environment that produces a happy and peaceful life.

Dogs care about all kinds of things, and although we can understand some of them, such as being afraid of thunderstorms, others are much more difficult to understand, such as being afraid of men with beards or people with hats.

Some dogs are naturally more fearful by nature and will always need much more peace of mind, but other dogs may feel anxious due to a bad experience.

The most obvious example of this is rescue dogs that are often anxious for the experience of being abandoned, and also for the unnatural situation in which they find themselves in a rescue center, which is full of other dogs.

Anxiety levels can be so extreme that a dog will shake or even hide at the mention of the word walk, and the slightest noise of thunder can make a dog foam in the mouth and run around the room.

Fireworks are another annual event that many dog owners believe is a test for their dog.

Sometimes, a dog's anxiety will only be a temporary problem and can be bought for things like health problems or an operation that leaves a dog more vulnerable for a while. This should go away when they start feeling better. In other cases, anxiety may arise gradually, for example, when dogs age.

CHAPTER THREE
SECRETS TO REDUCE DOG ANXIETY

Dog anxiety occurs due to certain factors. This emotion is demonstrated because your dog needs to communicate something. There is a feeling within him that must be addressed and the only suitable person to handle it is the owner and that's you! When dogs interact with other dogs, they have consolidated leadership. The leader provides direction and the group obeys and submits to the wishes of the leader. The positive of the dog's negative behavior is triggered by the feelings that the dog feels at that particular moment. It is important that you know that when the reasons for anxiety are addressed it immediately.

Secret #1: You have an important role in the development of anxiety

As mentioned, dogs are social and need leaders. You can never question the dog's obedience when leadership has been established. If your dog continues to exhibit unacceptable behavior despite continually reproaching him, something may be wrong in the way he was raised. You may not have established yourself as a strong leader who must be obeyed at any time. You may have shown some inconsistencies while previously trained. Firmness in the implementation of the rules is important.

Secret #2: The case is not hopeless; you can retrain your dog.

Some dog owners simply accept the fact that they can no longer do anything about continuous barking, chasing or chewing excessively. They only accept them as part of having a pet at home. This is not true. You can still do something about it. You can retrain your dog to change the wrong behavior. You just need time and enough attention to do it. However, it is worth doing to correct the problem.

Your role in your dog's life is very critical. The plan and program to be implemented must be reliable and effective. You should use a reference that can guarantee results that can be measured within certain time periods. This guide will address specific concerns and present strategies to correct the problem. The main secret of dealing with dog anxiety has to do with your knowledge of what's going on with your dog and also how to go about it.

CHAPTER FOUR
FIVE THINGS YOU SHOULD KNOW ABOUT DOG ANXIETY

Dogs experience anxiety and stress for several reasons. Whether it's a severe storm or a car trip, pet parents may be surprised to see that their furry friend has a serious and unexpected reaction.

Some dog breeds are subject to anxiety

Canine anxiety can affect any dog. But some races are genetically willing to experience anxiety.

Highly intelligent and high-energy breeds are more likely to develop this type of stress, such as Bernese mountain dogs, hunting dogs, cocker spaniels, German shepherds, Dalmatians, the great Pyrenees, the Pekingese, the Siberian husky, standard poodles, and some Terrier breeds.

Separation anxiety is a prevalent trigger among dogs

Dogs are very social animals. Along with noise and social anxiety, separation anxiety is one of the best types of stress that dogs develop. All dogs are at least attached to their owners to some extent, extreme stress when leaving home is a sign of anxiety. Dogs can start to react when they see it, just put on their jackets or take the keys.

Dogs express anxiety in various ways

While some dogs gasp or tremble in silence when they experience anxiety, others bark, chew and destroy furniture or defecate at home.

The range of symptoms dogs show when they feel anxious varies widely. Pet owners should pay attention to any atypical behavior that occurs when dogs are in different or new situations.

Training can help undo anxiety triggers

Just as a dog can be trained to sit and shake its paws, it can be unconditioned to unlearn phobias and anxiety triggers. Depending on the cause of the anxiety, you can evaluate exposures or routine actions that desensitize your dog.

Medications can help treat dogs with severe anxiety

In some cases, the use of tranquilizers or long-term medications is recommended to help dogs cope with severe anxiety. Dogs that have trouble flying or having fun with fireworks on July 4 may receive tranquilizers prescribed by a veterinarian. And puppies that are full of constant anxiety can be treated with regular medications. Thus this might seem like an easy alternative; I recommend you consider other options first.

Canine anxiety is stressful not only for dogs but also for their pet parents. But the right plan for diagnosis, treatment and behavior modification can help reduce anxiety almost immediately.

CHAPTER FIVE
EFFECTS OF ANXIETY ON THE HEALTH AND LIFE EXPECTANCY OF YOUR DOG

If you love your dog, take note, because recent research shows that fear and anxiety can affect your dog's health and shorten its lifespan. Then, along with the damage and destruction, you come home every time you leave your dog alone, or the constant barking and groans that push your neighbors against the wall or constant cleaning because your dog defecates and urinates at home while you are away, or even the concern it has at the first signs of a storm, we now have something else to worry about which is the effect it is having on the quality of life of our dog.

An increase in disease and a reduced lifespan

In other species, including people, it is already well studied and documented that the response to stress in situations that cause us to fear or anxiety is related to hormonal and immune system changes, which in turn are related to an increase in disease and reduced lifespan. A survey was conveyed to try to determine if the same was true for dogs. The investigation involved 721 owners of recently deceased dogs, who completed very detailed questionnaires, which were then analyzed to see if there were clear links between behavior, fear and anxiety, disease and causes of death.

Dogs that behave well live longer

The analysis found that well-behaved dogs lived longer. On the contrary, it has been shown that dogs with separation anxiety and other fears are more likely to have skin problems, in addition to having them more frequently and more severely.

In general, although research has not been able to directly correlate fear and anxiety with the cause of death in dogs, a dog's fear of strangers was correlated with a significantly reduced lifespan.

Quickly respond to dog anxiety problems

Two things stand out from this research. The first is that it will not help you or your dog to leave fear or anxiety problems unsolved. You really need to act immediately instead of leaving it in the hope that it will resolve itself or disappear over time.

The second is that a dog with good behavior will live longer, which is one of the best reasons I have been for a long time to persevere in training your dog. Remember, you will do it in your favor because, in the long run, you will live longer and healthier lives. And finally, think about how useful a happy dog will be and good behavior for your stress levels.

CHAPTER SIX
TYPES OF DOG ANXIETY

There are several types of dog anxiety. Identifying the type can help you understand what triggers your dog's anxiety attacks and, if possible, reduce, eliminate or block the stimulus or help your dog control anxiety. Dogs do not wake up one morning after deciding to be anxious or fearful. Most dogs that show symptoms of anxiety have had some events in the past that triggered anxiety. Dogs develop phobias and fears between 12 and 36 months or when they reach social maturity. If during this period, something triggers a strong fear reaction, they can develop a coherent anxiety pattern.

For instance, a dog that has had a car accident with its owner may be afraid to travel by car. Just approaching the car or the highway can cause the dog to tremble, bark, run, vomit or tremble. The dog connects the smells, panoramas, and sounds of cars and highways with the pain and fear of suffering a car accident. Other dogs may develop separation anxiety or other phobias during that period. Types of dog anxiety include:

Separation anxiety

Many dogs surrender to the kennel due to separation anxiety. The moans, barks, and destruction that accompanies this type of canine anxiety can be distressing, not only for you and your pet but also for neighbors who hear your dog howl for hours every day. Separation anxiety occurs when a dog becomes deeply attached to its pack, and in this case, it is you and your family.

Some people inadvertently create situations conducive to the development of canine separation anxiety by telling stories about their dog when they leave during the day or return at night. The dog begins to feel that something important is about to happen and shows symptoms of anxiety before his flock leaves for the day.

Separation anxiety in dogs can start from early childhood. Many owners of new dogs, distressed when they hear their puppy cry at night, pick it up, pamper it and generally worry about it. The puppy is experiencing his first time away from his mother and his littermates and quickly realizes that they complain, cry or bark. The puppy trains its owners to respond, not vice versa.

As the puppy becomes a dog, it also experiences less interaction with its owners. Puppies take a lot of time and training. Breaking in, walking on a leash and basic commands take time to learn. However, gradually, as a dog grows, its owners can spend less time exercising like this and simply expect the dog to behave. The dog still craves the company and can act to get it.

Social anxiety

Many people think that dogs love to play with other dogs. Some dogs, however, suffer from social anxiety. This type of canine anxiety manifests as aggressive behavior perceived around other dogs. Dogs that suffer from social anxiety do not understand the difference between friends and enemies. For them, each dog is a perceived threat. They strike first to avoid the threat. They can bark, throw themselves at other dogs or growl or explode them.

Some dogs with social anxiety behave in all unknown beings, both the person and the animal. They may feel comfortable with family members, but if someone comes unexpectedly to the door, the dog expresses his anxiety by growling or knocking at the stranger. Other dogs can be affectionate and calm with strangers and even with other animals, such as cats, but other dogs may be deeply anxious and scared.

It is believed that the cause of social anxiety in dogs is early weaning or the elimination of their mothers' puppies too soon. Since the dog has not had the opportunity to understand how other dogs interact, being with other dogs makes him feel anxious. The dog never got to know that other dogs could be friends. Puppies must be at least 8-weeks old before mothers and littermates take them away to wean them. The first 8-weeks of a puppy's life is a crucial time for him to learn social skills. Playing with their littermates, fighting with mom and enjoying life with their pack helps dogs understand how other dogs communicate and interact. Without this time together, dogs are afraid of other dogs. Other dogs become an unknown and frightening entity.

*_Noise anxiety_*

This is another common type of dog anxiety. Many dogs are afraid of loud or sudden noises. The bursting of thunder or the rise of fireworks is enough to make them frantic. Dogs also begin to connect other physical signs with noise. They can perceive the changes in barometric pressure that precedes a storm. Even windy days can cause dizziness since most thunderstorms are accompanied by winds.

CHAPTER SEVEN
DEALING WITH DOG SEPARATION ANXIETY

One of the common phrases used by dog owners to describe a dog that seems stressed when the owner leaves the house, or simply leaves the room, is the anxiety about separation in dogs. We can define separation anxiety as a problematic behavior of the dog that manifests itself through symptoms such as excessive salivation, barking, groans, destruction of objects in the house, scratches on the walls, doors, and floors and trying to escape from the box or the room.

Simulated separation anxiety vs. real separation anxiety

There is real separation anxiety and simulated separation anxiety, where the dog's behavior seems to be separation anxiety, but in reality, it is a learned behavior. Simulated separation anxiety often occurs when the dog lacks leadership and self-control. True anxiety about separation, on the other hand, makes the dog feel real stress during the absence of his master.

In simulated separation anxiety, the dog knows he will receive attention if he misbehaves. For some dogs, being reprimanded verbally for such behavior is also gratifying because they feel noticed. Negative attention can be a reward in a lot of cases if the dog owner is not aware that some of your dog's needs are not being met. In cases like these, there is little real stress involved, just bad behavior.

Simulated separation anxiety is quite easy to overcome with a gradual approach, which slowly increases the amount of time he/she spends in the crate, both when you are at home and away from it, constant obedience training, adequate amounts of exercise and leadership. Severe cases of true separation anxiety represent a challenge for the leaders of the pack.

__Causes of dog separation anxiety__

Dog separation anxiety is often encouraged without knowing it by owners. We literally make a big fuss when we leave or go home, and in doing so, we reward the dog's concern with our absence, causing even more stress every time we leave. We love that our dogs are with us and when they are puppies, we take them everywhere to socialize. So, we have to leave them alone, but they reach an age when they not only want but also feel the need to be with us: we are their source of trust, their security and their package.

A change in your routine can create symptoms of separation anxiety from the dog, but destruction and stress can also be created by boredom and lack of exercise. Terriers are born to dig, protective breeds to protect and retrieve to carry. So, in some cases, we are holding them back from their instincts and impulses, instead of feeding them.

Remember these words, which I consider a good start to correct these problems: "exercise, discipline and only then, affection." You need to find a balance between patience, obedience, and trust in your dog. Try to develop a behavior in our dog that reflects the harmonious collaboration that both shares. He must have enough confidence in himself and in your leadership. In this way, he can rely on situations, such as staying alone, because he knows that you will always provide the necessary. He trusts and understands that you will come back home.

How to deal with dog separation anxiety

Veterinarians may prescribe medications, which tend to calm a dog's senses, but they are not a cure. Medications only provide a support mechanism to help the owner rehabilitate the dog; it is only a temporary solution to the underlying problem. You have to deal with the root cause. It really starts the moment you pick up your puppy. Too often, puppies are taken from the litter begins to cry when left alone. This is a great change for the puppy; they no longer have the package they were born with. When he cries, we will look for him and show sympathy: his crying is rewarded. Later, if he cries in the crate, and you let him out, he is rewarded for his crying. Reward only the desired behavior.

From the beginning, we must teach our puppy to shut up and calm down for increasing periods of time. We have to teach patience and calm and reward it instead. When he is with us, we shouldn't be trying to constantly interact with him.

Let him learn to have fun with his toys. Teach the puppy to accept the crate. Allow him to explore under the supervision and learn the limits and boundaries of his surroundings; to gain respect for this environment and for the people in it. This means consistency in all the things you do and includes all family members that interact with your dog.

The importance of discipline and obedience training

I believe that much of the cure for separation anxiety comes from discipline and obedience training. This approach allows your dog to know what is expected of him, which helps his good behavior become a habit. You feel bad about showing unwanted behavior, even without your indication. Take advantage of that.

Pass the training, not just the lessons once a week, often and steadily. Show him dog what you want from him in/around the house and during daily routines. Two minutes here, five minutes there. Not only go for a walk but train while sitting on the sidewalk and sitting when you meet other people, people, and dogs.

Teach your dog to sit in front of the door, lie down and stay out of sight for increasing periods of time in your home.

Train your dog to sit down and wait for the guests to receive him, getaway when you go to the refrigerator and go to the bathroom at the right time. In general, you should teach your dog in small steps to be respectful and self-confident. Rehabilitation begins by letting your dog understands what is expected of him. You and every other member of your family are the leaders of the pack and should be recognized as such, not as dictators, but as leaders.

For example, if your dog approaches you and pushes you or hits you with its paw. You think he is cute and caressed. This becomes a habit, and your dog now thinks, "I have control and can tell you what to do." So, when he can't do it, he gets anxious.

Crate training to avoid separation anxiety

When you are at home, make sure your dog is familiar with being in the cage. Start with short a period of time and then increase the time you spend there. Feed him in the crate and then let him have his favorite bone to use as anti-stress while there. Some toys are designed to entertain or occupy your dog when you are not there. I prefer to use these interactive toys only when I am present. They work because your dog's mind is stimulated while trying to remove the delights of a toy, which then relaxes his mind and sleeps.

Do not put water in the crate; it could get very messy! The crate should be your dog's safe spot, a place where he feels safe and enjoys. It must be large enough to stand without the head touching the top and must be able to turn and lie down easily.

If it barks in the crate, look for ways to check. Teaching him "quiet" is good and stops barking so he learns that there is no reward for what works. In extreme cases, a proper bark collar can help control the dog's bark in its absence. Nobody wants annoying neighbors and this device will correct it when you're not there.

When you leave it, do it in silence and don't give ideas. Don't say anything. Follow your silent start routine, pick up car keys, open garage doors and start the car. Then, return inside without paying attention to your dog. Do what you always do when you go out: play role-playing games if it helps you. Go back home and don't pay attention to your dog. Pass by him, say hello and smile if he's quiet, but if he comes charging towards you, ignore him and leave.

Waits for him to stay calm, then ask him to wait in the crate while you open the door. He shouldn't come rushing at you. If you realize an action, such as putting on a pair of shoes, picking up your car keys, going to a certain door, causing stress, then do that action and don't leave. Let him know so much about the action that he accepts it.

Place the crate in the busiest room in the home. The goal is for your dog to accept all normal movements, noises and daily events inside your home. Your dog should realize that he doesn't need to get involved in everything because you are the manager. You can have more than one crate if you want to. For instance, you want your friend to sleep in the room next to your bed. Covering the crate with a sheet when it comes out gives the feeling of a den and your dog could better appreciate the crate in this way.

All my dogs love music and television, so I leave it for them. It provides a familiar and visual background sound for them, giving them a sense of security.

Change your routine

It is possible that your dog recognizes a series of actions; you must be intelligent. Changing your dog's habits often means changing yours and this can be difficult, we are habitual creatures, but you will have to change your routine.

Use a different door, put your coat and bag in different places. Make your changes to create a different image. If you are watching TV or working on the computer and your dog gets up every time he gets up, just get up and sit down again.

Your dog doesn't have to follow you everywhere. Yes, he can look, but he should be able to wait until you ask for his company. These small changes will help teach your dog to have the self-confidence he needs to handle loneliness. The separation anxiety can be overcome; it can make some dogs run quite quickly, while others require time, patience and consistency.

Exercise, obedience, and lifestyle; I said rules, limits, and boundaries, all of which are necessary for a balanced dog. The consistency of you and each human being in your family will also be crucial to increase your dog's confidence in you as leader of the pack but also in himself.

Ten steps to prevent separation anxiety

The most important ingredient in an effective separation anxiety prevention program is to prepare your dog for success. When you bring a new dog home, implement a program to help you feel comfortable for yourself during gradually increasing periods. This will help ensure that there is no need to panic: showing you have not abandoned him and you always come back. Make sure you exercise him well before practicing; A tired dog is a much better candidate for relaxation than one who is "full" of energy.

These are the ten steps of a two-day program to create a dog that feels comfortable being alone. Note that if you are modifying an existing anxiety condition, you will have to follow the phases of the program much more slowly.

Step #1: Bring your dog home at a time when someone can spend a few days with him to relieve the stress of the transition.

Step #2: Prepare a quiet and safe space, such as a crate or a pen for puppies or a dog-proof room, such as a laundry room in advance.

Step #3: When you bring your dog home, give him the opportunity to free himself outdoors and spend 10 to 15 minutes with him at home under close supervision. Put it in your pen and stay in the room with him.

Step #4: Stay close first. Read a book. If he gets excited, ignore it. When he is quiet, say goodbye calmly, step forward and then come back before he has a chance to get angry. Talk to him calmly, then read again. You are teaching him that if you leave, you will return. Other family members are expected to be scarce during this time: your dog must learn to be alone.

Step #5: Continue moving away from time to time, gradually increasing the distance and varying the time you are away so that you can eventually walk around the room without disturbing your dog. Every time you come back, greet him calmly. Occasionally say, "Yes!" With a calm but cheerful voice before returning to him, then return to the pen and feed him.

Step #6: After about an hour, give it a rest. Take it out of the bathroom and play. Get out a little. Then go back inside and resume the exercises with the pen.

Step #7: Start over, staying close to the pen until it settles. This time, more quickly, follow steps 4 and 5 until you can tour the room without generating an alarm. Now step in another room very briefly and come back before your dog has time to get anxious. Gradually increase the time you stay outside the room, alternating between wandering around the room, sitting next to him, reading a book and sitting in front of him. If he starts to worry, wait until he stops worrying, then returns. Teach him that calm behavior brings you back and, restlessness keeps you away.

Step #8: Occasionally, leave the house. Your goal for the first day is to reassure your dog with you that is away from him for 15-20 minutes; usually, the first 20 minutes of separation is more difficult. Vary your times, so he doesn't start anticipating your return. Remember to give him a bag to go to the bathroom and take breaks: every hour for a young puppy, every hour or two for a bigger dog.

Step #9: On the second day, repeat the warm-up steps quickly, until it is not possible to leave for 15-20 minutes in a row, interspersed with shorter separations. During one of your outdoor excursions, get in the car and drive around the block. Return between 5 and 10 minutes and calmly return to the house as it was during the rest of the exercises. Spend some time, then go out and run again, for half an hour this time.

Step #10: Now is the time for Sunday brunch. Make sure your dog has a complete rest and a game, then give him 15 minutes to relax after stimulating the game. Put a Kong full of delicious treats in his pen, gather the family and leave the house in silence for a trip of a couple of hours. When you get home from a calm and happy dog, have a toast with orange juice at your graduation from separation anxiety prevention school.

There is a limit to the dog-alone time

It is not fair to ask a young dog to stay home alone for 5-10 hours. He needs to leave to free himself in the middle of the day. If you force him to get dirty at home, in the worst case, you can cause stress-related behaviors, at best, you could create training problems at home. Options may include taking him to work with you, having family members return home at lunchtime, arranging for neighbors to stay home to take him out, hiring a walker to accompany him and playing with him or send it to a well-managed dog care environment. If you establish a routine to help your dog succeed, one day, you will get your Master in Dog Home-Alone and trust the total freedom of the house. It may be too late for some dog owners to say they have never had a dog with separation anxiety, but it is never too late to say, "Never again"!

Tips to help dog separation anxiety

Imagine going back home from a long day at work to a whirlwind of energy that goes round and round. Your dog follows you to your living room, where you discover that he has chewed your favorite shoes. Your neighbor comes to tell you that, once again, your dog went crazy in the neighborhood howling and barking while you were gone. Is this scenario familiar? Your dog may suffer separation anxiety. Naturally, dogs are almost never far from their pack. Our job is to help make this unnatural situation less stressful! Here are a few tips to relieve separation anxiety:

Tip #1: Take your dog for a walk before leaving the house

Start the day by taking your dog for a quick walk. To make the walk more rigorous, use a backpack for extra-weight dogs.

So, reward your dog's calm energy with food and water. Some dogs may have to rest before eating, but all dogs may benefit from hydration. The idea is to leave the dog in a silent and quiet mode while away.

Tip #2: No contact, no speech, no eye contact

Do not do much when you leave for the day or when you return. In this way, you are telling your dog that separation time is no big deal. It's just business as usual! Depending on the severity of the dog's anxiety, it may be necessary to practice the period for five minutes or up to an hour before leaving and when you return.

Tip #3: Say goodbye to your dog long before you leave

Do you have difficulty practicing "without contact, without speech, without eye contact"? Take a moment to show affection and tell your dog that you will miss him long before you leave. Keep in mind that this screen is for you, not for your dog! Your dog will not suffer his feelings if you don't greet him.

Tip #4: Keep calm and determination

When you are ready to leave for work, leave those feelings of guilt, nerves and worry behind. Instead, let your dog know that everything will be fine by projecting the safe energy of a pack leader.

A calm and determined leader can relieve separation anxiety in dogs.

Tip #5. Start with something small like leaving your dog alone for five minutes

Leave your dog alone for at least five minutes and then extend the time to twenty minutes, then an hour. Keep increasing the time you spend until you can leave for eight hours without further problems with the dog!

Tip #6. Leave your dog with a good audiobook

Reports have now shown that audiobooks can have a calming effect on dogs and help reduce separation anxiety. The sound of a human voice can help reduce your stress while you are not at home.

CHAPTER EIGHT
DEALING WITH SOCIAL ANXIETY

Some dogs may experience anxiety or fear in social situations. It can happen when you take the dog to the park, walk in the crowd, go to the vet or even visit your friends' houses. Proper socialization is essential for all dogs. The lack of socialization can result in a dog with paralyzing social anxiety, fear and sometimes even aggression. Many people do not realize how a lack of socialization can affect the behavior of their pets, although there are steps you can take to help your puppy feel more comfortable.

What is social anxiety?

Social anxiety in dogs is the fear of people, other animals or places, places, sounds and other stimuli unknown in the environment. A dog can feel perfectly comfortable with members of its human family and, therefore, feel anxious with strangers, for example. Similarly, some go well inside or in their territory, but panic when they leave the house. Depending on the dog, the degree of anxiety in a social environment can be mild or extreme. It can make a dog act or behave in ways that are not normally observed in a family environment.

Signs of social anxiety in dogs

While some dogs may become very shy, others may feel trapped and cornered, which often causes fearful aggression. When a dog with its back against the wall experiences the biological fight or flight response, the only action available is to fight.

- Aggressive behavior, such as barking, grunting or jumping towards a person or animal.

- Shy and scary behavior, including snuggling behind the owner, complaining or even screaming.

- Some dogs show signs of extreme nervousness, such as gasping or drooling. They may also urinate or defecate suddenly without seeming to know.

Causes of social anxiety

Puppies who are not presented with new experiences may feel overwhelmed when they meet new people or dogs. They can also get nervous on the way or to the park because it is simply too much to take it all at once.

Proper socialization at an early age can help them learn to adapt to new situations throughout their lives. Adult dogs may also experience social anxiety. It is more common in dogs rescued from puppy farms or in offensive and negligent situations.

They may have had little or no contact with people or only negative experiences with people.

Stray dogs may be more anxious because they have a distrust of people and busy places. This could be something they learned that was necessary to survive on the street. Dogs that grow in rural areas or are protected in their homes and rarely leave can get very scared when they are taken out of their territory.

How to deal with social anxiety

If your dog is anxious, you must be careful to overcome fear. It is best to start small and desensitize a scary dog is hard work. This can be a long process that can take weeks or months, but it is worth it. You should carefully evaluate how much your dog can handle simultaneously. Be patient and keep it positive. Start by letting your dog know one person at a time. Allow your dog to make contact and make sure he has a safe shelter where he can go if he begins to feel overwhelmed. Remember, go slowly, reward good behavior and moments when it is calm. Do not comfort the dog when he is scared, as this can reinforce terrifying behavior instead of helping the dog overcome it.

Through constant exposure to new experiences, you should keep in mind that your dog relaxes more as things become more familiar.

Make each trip fun. If you take the dog to a busy street and it is scary, end the tour in a place you like, for example, a quiet park to play or a walk in a quiet street. This way, the dog is less likely to be afraid of travel in general. While it is possible that your dog never learns to love being in busy areas, he can learn to tolerate them if, in the end, you can associate the exits with the "good part."

If your dog is anxious with other dogs, be sure to keep him away from dogs when he is not in control of the situation. Avoid dog parks and cross the street while walking if another dog comes to you. When you choose to introduce your dog to other dogs, do it very slowly and carefully. Choose a calm and detached dog that does not seem threatening to your dog, stay a comfortable distance and limit it to a short time. Reward your dog for his calm behavior. If the dog remains calm, it is possible to gradually reduce the distance between the dogs and increase the exposure time. At the first subtle sign of anxiety, increase the distance between the two dogs or completely take your dog away if necessary.

The goal here is to prevent anxiety from accumulating at a high level. Your dog may never learn to appreciate the company of other dogs. However, he can learn to tolerate the presence of another remote dog.

How to prevent social anxiety

Socialization is more successful when it starts early. Begin the puppy's socialization process as soon as possible. This essentially trains your dog to deal with demanding situations. A well-socialized dog does not fear the crowd and plays well with other dogs; socializing puppies is the only period in a dog's life in which you can change and create most of the dog's behaviors that will remain with him throughout his life. Basically, you can completely model your dog's vision of the surrounding world and how he will react to it and behave in it.

Do you know that during the period of socialization of puppies, can even manage (or completely change) the instinct and driving of a dog? Now, you may be wondering something like this; "Why should I know?" The answer is very simple: you have no choice! There are two ways in which your dog will grow from your puppy's socialization period to become a matured dog: With your input and your guide. Do you have a well-behaved dog that will be a worthy part of the family and community? Or your dog will conceive behavior patterns on his own and he will have to deal with them at some point in life. Coping with established behavior patterns will take time, investment and there is no guarantee that it will succeed.

So, how much time do you have?

Puppy in the appearance of about 16 weeks; by the sixteenth week, approximately 85% of a dog's brain develops and the puppy's socialization window is almost closed.

What your dog has not learned or familiarized at this time will become a problem along the way. At that point, it will become a long and slow process to repair/adapt it and, as mentioned, in some cases, it would be impossible to overcome it completely.

How easy is it to make mistakes during puppy socialization?

In today's world, there are a lot of information on how to properly socialize puppies, but unfortunately, most of that information is based on obsolete concepts that tell you to keep your puppy away from everything until he is around six months or more (which will probably create fear-related behaviors) or invest your time in nurseries for overcrowded puppies or supervised dog parks where your dog will simply become classic to be overexcited every time he sees another dog.

The same goes for your dog's reactions to other people; improper exposure can create an aggressive dog; however, inappropriate exposure will create a dog that will get excited every time you see someone on the street.

Where to start

Puppy Development

This is a step-by-step guide to the early stages and stages of socializing the puppies. Many people do not know that the first steps are taken shortly after the birth of the puppy (in the neonatal phase) and continue from there. Here you can find out what are the duties of responsible breeders and how many problems can be created before the first six weeks of your dog's life. What are your first steps as a dog owner?

Puppies and distractions

This is one of the most important steps in your dog's life. How it will deal with distractions and the world in general. Dogs are animals completely different from humans and have different relationships and visions of the world of us. If you omit this important step with your dog and do not create behavioral patterns that you like, the dog will create its own behaviors during the socialization phase of the puppies.

If your dog ends up with dysfunctional behaviors towards the environment, he will have partial and limited success in solving them along the way. To start with the right foot, click here!

Puppy Playtime

The game is one of the most important aspects of a dog's life. It is much more than a simple game; It is a kind of language. Playing with your puppy is much more than being dumb.

The purpose of the toys

Playing with your pup is the first step in building a strong relationship during the period of socialization of the puppy and lasts the lifetime of your dog.

Ideas to socialize puppies, tips and practical training plans

We have all heard about and we practically have an opinion on what and how the pups' socialization should be. Do you know what is "location" or "attachment"? These are a normal part of the socialization exercise in which you teach your dog how to see the world and where you teach him self-control and how to create certain responses to certain situations.

Start by taking your puppy to different places. It is better to do this after it has been completely immunized. By exposing the dog when he is young to different places, sounds and people, you teach him to accept them as usual. You will have a happy and friendly dog that handles others well.

If you adopt an adult dog, you cannot be sure of what you have been exposed to. Don't worry; you can still socialize an adult dog. You should begin this process as soon as you bring your new dog home. Dealing with dogs that have lost adequate socialization during the period of socialization of the puppy and now show what we call "dysfunctional behavior patterns" falls under the umbrella of behavior modification. Some dog trainers also try corrective socialization.

Remedial socialization

Remedial socialization is basically a different term for exercises in which the principles of desensitization and counterconditioning are used.

How much can remedial socialization help?

This depends on the problem and the dog itself. If you are dealing with a dog that exhibits a pattern of behavior in some situations that you would like to address. Social anxiety in dogs is often described as dogs that feel uncomfortable when exposed to social situations.

Dogs can often feel intimidated when they are close to people or other animals. Nervous behavior can be exhibited when barking and growling when exposed to new people or dogs. This is often a behavior that increases distance, which means that the dog expects to increase the distance. The dog tells the person, "Please stay away; I don't feel comfortable with you." Some other dogs hide and hide behind the owner. There are also cases of terrified screaming dogs as if they were dying when another dog approached them. Many small dogs feel better when they are picked up.

Social anxiety in dogs towards people

Many dogs perform well with people they already know and have trusted as caregivers, but they have problems with people they don't know.

For dogs with social anxiety for people they don't know, it is important to help them understand that they are safe with other people and those good things happen when there are people nearby. How can we communicate it to our dogs?

This requires desensitization and counter-conditioning. For example, if you have a dog that barks and growls when people enter the house, you would use a program similar to this "how to prevent my dog from barking when someone enters the room." If your dog experiences social anxiety while walking when people approach, you can apply a protocol similar to the one presented in the section on social anxiety in dogs towards dogs. Keep in mind that, for security and correct implementation, it would be ideal to hire a professional to help you.

There are a lot of things to keep in mind when changing dog behavior and strength-free professionals are the best source to rely on to receive the best guidance and reduce dog stress.

Social anxiety in dogs towards dogs

Social anxiety in dogs can cause lungs and barking. If your dog responds to other dogs, you can use a program that includes desensitization and counterconditioning.

There are several programs, but one of my favorites is LAT by Leslie McDevitt. Here is a description of the program: Change the behavior of dogs through LAT. Dragging your dog away from other dogs during the walks to prevent the dog from stretching and barking will not do much because you have to deal with the underlying emotions. It could be a good management tool to make a quick turn and redirect your dog towards you to pay attention.

It is important to increase the distance with dogs that create anxiety so that your dog is not so stressed while walking. This requires time and gradual work in controlled contexts.

Training an emergency reversal is always a good idea for those times when you are not prepared and want to leave the area. When gradually introducing dogs to the stimuli that make them feel uncomfortable, it is important to be careful not to overcome them. Also, since dogs are at the limit when they are exposed to stimuli with which they are not comfortable, you may need to find treats that are at the top of your dog's reward hierarchy.

Therefore, to help your dog walk, you must first find his comfort level, a distance from which he does not exceed the threshold and from there, start working on the LAT exercises.

<u>The world is unpredictable out there</u>

Even with your best effort, the world is never predictable, and a dog can get out of nowhere, causing setbacks in its progress. Even with guests or strangers, your dog can do well until the guests sneeze or the stranger approaches their dog. A good option will be to initially enroll your dog in a mobile reagent class in your area if you have a dog trainer that offers it. In a reactive Rover class, the trainer can measure distance and work with dogs that act as "stimulus dogs" that are calm dogs that can help your dog calm down and be better equipped to overcome his fears.

CHAPTER NINE
DEALING WITH DOG NOISE ANXIETY

Dog noise anxiety can occur in response to any type of loud noise, including fireworks, thunderstorms, shots, sirens, alarms, electronic noises, speakers, vacuum cleaners and more. The level of fear that a dog feels/shows can vary from mild nervousness to total panic and everything else. There are millions of dogs in the United States that suffer some degree of noise anxiety, and their owners also suffer because it is horrible to see their pet so scared.

Dog noise anxiety may gradually get worse over time if it is not addressed/treated; it even becomes a phobia. A dog with a noise phobia may begin to fear a noise, like thunder, but over time the phobia spreads to other loud noises until it jumps with each sound. It is not a fun way to live at all. There are somethings you can do to help your dog if he is afraid of loud noises and the sooner he starts, the better.

Causes of dog noise anxiety

Dog's fear of loud noises can be as a result of several things. First, it is actually a normal reaction to be afraid of something we do not understand or jump into a sudden and unexpected noise. Dogs do not understand what thunder is, because fireworks light up the sky or because the monster with a loud and scary voice (also known as the vacuum cleaner) goes crazy in your home. But not all dogs are scared of loud noises. Individual temperament plays an important role. The same goes for genetics. If a dog has a marked fear (or phobia) of loud noises, puppies are likely to have the same fear as well. Not all puppies, but some. Genetics is a kind of lottery like that.

Proper socialization as a young pup also plays a role in the trust (or fear) of a dog as the puppy grows. Puppies that are not exposed to a wide range of people, pets, experiences, and environments are often more anxious and fearful in general since they have never had the opportunity to build self-confidence outside of their daily environment/routine. Sometimes, anxiety is triggered by a stressful or unpleasant experience. Everything that is related (in the dog's brain) to this experience becomes something that you may be afraid of in the future. Maybe for life. Phobias can arise this way!

Anxiety, fear and phobia are different

There is a difference between fear, anxiety and phobia. The definition of each one's dictionary is:

- Anxiety: a persistent feeling of worry or discomfort about something that may not have happened yet or that has an uncertain outcome.

- Fear: this is an unpleasant emotion caused by the threat of danger, pain or damage.

- Phobia: an extreme or irrational fear or aversion to something

Anxiety is often associated with something that can happen, a vague sense of worry that can be chronic. Fear is a helpful biological reaction to a situation that puts us in danger and is designed to protect us. Phobias are usually irrational and extreme fears that are totally disproportionate to the object of that fear. Shepherd dogs are more likely to fear loud noises than others. It is a race-specific genetic trait. These include the Australian Shepherd, the Border Collie, the German Shepherd, the Golden Retriever, the former English Shepherd, the Pembroke Welsh Corgi (yes, the Corgis may be small but originally raised for cattle raising), the Shetland sheepdog. Some of these races can be reactive above average, high energy, super intelligent and tend to be nervous.

Other anxiety-related behaviors, such as separation anxiety or obsessive-compulsive behaviors, such as hoop or tail hunting, may also be more common in these races. Dogs that are truly phobic (rather than just anxious) for one thing can also have excessive reactions to others.

Dog scared by the storm

Older dogs may be more anxious in general and may begin to fear things that do not bother them when they were younger. Lack of vision and/or hearing or a decrease in robust physical health contribute to this as the world becomes a more difficult place to negotiate. A dog that has pain or anguish from a physical condition, or an emotional one, probably responds better to any kind of stimulus, including noise.

So, if your dog does not feel well, is recovering from surgery or a shocking experience or is anxious about changes in his life, then he is more likely to show signs of noise, anxiety.

Symptoms of dog noise anxiety

The signs that your dog is scared of thunder, fireworks or, in general, worries about loud noises can be very varied. All dogs are different and may also react differently to the same types of fears. The signs of fear shown by your dog will also vary according to the degree of fear. Anxiety will lead to a much less severe reaction than a phobia. These are the most common signs of fear in dogs.

- Trembling
- Sticky and velcro behavior of the dog
- Panting, yawning, drooling
- Stimulation

- Tail down, ears back, eyes wide open

- Hide or try to escape

- Curled up, inability to move, catatonic

- Complain, bark, howl

- Chew, dig, scratch and destructive behaviors.

- Loss of control of the bladder and intestine.

- Your dog can show one or two of them or most of them.

A dog that is anxious or slightly fearful may simply be stickier than usual, shaking or shaking and moaning from time to time. A dog with noise phobia can run frantically, drool excessively, lose control of its bodily functions and be so desperate to escape the noise that breaks a window or destroys the door.

Dogs Noise anxiety therapy

The treatment of anxiety by dog noise implies a double approach: comfort and desensitization. Comfort involves controlling anxiety for the dog so he can reduce his frightening reactions and help him feel less scared. Desensitization can help your dog overcome and eventually eliminate those fears by gradually exposing him to things by combining his exposure to things he fears with pleasant experiences/rewards.

Comforting a dog with noise anxiety

Since each individual dog is different in the way it shows its fear and what it seeks for its comfort, there is no single method to comfort a dog with noise anxiety. You will have to look at your dog and see what he does to try to console himself first.

- Does he hold on? Does he want to be loved and reassured?

- Run to the dog's cage or bed.

- Does he try to reach the bottom of a closet or crawl under the bed?

- Does he cry, chew, dig or run frantically?

Each reaction helps you see what kind of comfort your dog naturally seeks to feel less fear. This is what you can do to help you get maximum comfort for him.

Give love and attention

If being close to you is what your dog wants to feel safe when he is afraid, then that is what you should allow him to have. But this can be counter-productive if you comfort him in a way that reinforces his fear instead of reducing it. When trying to comfort a dog with noise anxiety, do not use a "baby" voice or act as if you had a reason to be afraid. Don't hold him tight and hum: "Oh, poor doggy, I'm so sorry that a loud thunder scares you."

Instead, use a bright and optimistic voice and a very practical approach.

Try saying something like, "I'm sorry you're afraid, but it's okay, let's sit on the couch and watch TV together." Do you see the difference? Try it, use voices and word sets and you will understand what I mean. Distraction is important. Try to distract him from whatever it is that is causing your dog's anxiety. Let him chew a Kong full of his favorite delicacies or a tasty bone that he only gets on special occasions with you.

Or maybe a hide and seek game or an interactive game or puzzle. Having a special time with you will be a pleasure for him. Obviously, this only works for anxious or slightly fearful dogs, absolute terror or phobia does not respond to logic, since it is a primitive behavior based on fear.

Help him find his "safe spot."

Sometimes anxiety about the dog's noise anxiety can cause your dog to run and hide in the smallest and darkest place he can find or in a place where he feels safer.

This could be his crate (in which case, throwing a light blanket over it can make you feel even safer) or under a bed or table. It could also be in a closet or in a smaller bathroom. Your dog knows what he needs, so it is better to leave it hidden where he feels most comfortable.

If getting to your safe place makes it less frightening, then all you have to do is make it as comfortable as possible and most likely leave it alone. Some dogs feel better about their owner right next to them. Others prefer to be alone. You will know which one your dog wants. Try to find out if your dog feels better in the dark or in the light, or perhaps with a low-power table lamp or nightlight is what he feels most comfortable with. Sometimes, putting cotton balls in your dog's ears can help muffle the loud noises they fear so much.

Products that can help reduce noise anxiety

There are a lot of different products that can help dogs suffering from noise anxiety. These include natural remedies and supplements, physical products and anti-anxiety medications. These are some of the most popular options of natural anti-anxiety products for dogs:

Pheromone products

Pheromone products use naturally occurring pheromone flavors to help calm anxious dogs and puppies. They are available as necklaces, room diffusers and aerosols. The positive aspects are that pheromone products are completely natural, have no side effects and can be extremely effective for small and medium dogs and puppies.

The disadvantages are that it is not an "instant solution," pheromone products often take between 12 and 36 hours to begin to be effective and that for larger dogs, a collar may just not be enough. However, if your dog hates fireworks, it is a good idea to install a pheromone diffuser in the room where your chest is (or safe place) and place a pheromone collar several days before the fireworks are about to start. Other remedies/natural products that help reduce anxiety and have a calming effect include the Jacksons Galaxy Stress Cap, Bach's Pet Rescue Remedy, Hemp Calming Help and HomeoPet Storm Stress for dogs.

Physical products

Physical products that can reduce the symptoms of dog noise anxiety include: Wraps, shirts or coats designed to apply gentle and soothing pressure to your dog's body.

These work with the same principle of wrapping a baby. There are several to choose from. The best-known brand is the Thundershirt. The American Kennel Club also offers its AKC anti-stress and anti-stress soothing coat and the adjustable pet wrap and anti-stress coat.

Music

Then there is music, which can be as relaxing for dogs as it is for people. Classical or meditation soundtracks have proven effective in reducing stress in dogs and there are several CDs available that have been designed specifically for our canine companions. You can find a range of these on this CD page for dog relaxation.

Medications

Drug options for drug noise anxiety include: Sileo is the first FDA-approved medication for dogs suffering from noise anxiety. T

his innovative medicine was launched in 2016 and worked by blocking the chemical norepinephrine in the brain. Stressful situations cause the body to release high levels of norepinephrine to mobilize the fight or flight mechanism and these high levels cause symptoms and anxiety reactions. During the tests and the evaluation, Sileo was said to be "impressive" and reduces anxiety without sedating the dog, so he will act normally but will not be afraid. Gel form easy to administer and effective for up to three hours with very few side effects.

Your veterinarian may prescribe Sileo for anxiety about dog noise and you may find it cheaper to buy Sileo online. It is always worth checking. Another drug that the veterinarian can prescribe is Clomicalm. It is usually used to treat separation anxiety in dogs, but it can also be used to treat anxiety problems from dog noise. Other drugs that are often used to treat dog noise anxiety include medications for humans such as Xanax, Prozac and the like.

Desensitizing your dog to loud noises

Life, in general, can be very loud and many dogs find loud and frightening noises. Desensitizing your dog to loud noises is a good way to keep him calm in situations that might otherwise make him anxious. While there are several things you can do to calm your dog in loud noises, such as fireworks or bonfire nights, getting your dog used to loud sounds can be a better long-term solution. By gradually desensitizing your dog to loud noises over a certain period of time, you can teach him to associate these sounds with something positive, rather than something to fear.

This process must take place over a gradual period of time and can take months. Desensitization can be difficult to perform and, due to the way it works, there is the potential to make things worse. But if you go about it the right way, you can eliminate your dogs from the fear of loud noises instead of manipulating them (as you are doing with the comfort options above). In my personal opinion, if your dog has a strong anxiety about dog noise or a phobia of loud noises, it is worth the effort and the risk of trying it.

How to desensitize dog's with noise anxiety

First, you will need a CD or an audio recording of the specific noises that scare your dog. You can find them online quite easily, even for shooting, traffic fires, etc. Choose a time when your dog is calm and calm and start playing the CD for him at a volume low enough not to scare him.

Dogs generally have very sensitive ears, so the volume you need may be less than expected. Play the CD for approximately 10 minutes, then turn it off and treat your dog with a favorite treatment (or two) to remain calm.

Do this for about five days or so, then, on the sixth day, increase the volume slightly, always within the range that is comfortable for you. Repeat the cycle, then repeat again. For a few weeks (or maybe months, depending on how anxious you are) to increase the volume a little every 4 or 5 days and reward it delicately, you should be able to make it tolerate the noise that used to terrify you.

It is important to move to the rhythm of your dog and not scare him. Never force him to listen to a volume that makes him anxious, even if it takes two weeks to climb a couple of points. If he ever begins to show fear, reduce the volume again and then start increasing it only when he is comfortable again. You should be able to take it to a point where it is no longer afraid of its own rhythm. If you are exposed to the noise that scares him during that time, this could hinder your progress, even return to the starting point.

So, if it is a fear of the electrical storms that your dog suffers, try desensitizing it before the storm season (usually during spring and autumn). If you are afraid of the fireworks you fear, use the periods between New Year and July 4th to work on your desensitization.

Make your dog less stress from loud noises

This is probably very similar to what I talked about earlier. Before you begin, you should buy or transmit some sound effects or related noises, such as fireworks, and have a way to play them out loud. It is important that the training is done with your dog indoors, away from distractions, and make sure that your dog can easily leave the room if you wish.

To begin, have your dog settle in the room and reproduce the sounds that are least afraid of the smallest possible volume. Turn up the volume very, very slowly, until you see the first signs that your dog is reacting to noise. A reaction can be small, such as shaking the ears. Once your dog begins to react, leave the sounds at that volume for a few minutes to get used.

If at any time your dog is scared or stressed by noise, keep calm and stop playing sounds immediately. This means that you may have proceeded too quickly, so start with a lower volume next time. Play the sounds for 5-10 minutes, 3-4 times a day. Once your dog has gotten used to the noise, you can increase the volume slightly, until it starts responding again. Again, if your dog shows signs of stress, stop the sounds and start at a lower volume the next day. Keep playing sounds like this every day, for a period of weeks, until your dog no longer reacts to the sounds, even at a higher volume.

Develop a positive association between your dog and noises

Once your dog has become numb to sounds, you can begin to build a positive association between your dog and loud noises, such as fireworks. To start, prepare your dog's food or take out one of his toys. If they get excited, sit quietly for a few minutes and let them rest before starting the training session. Once the dog has calmed down, play the sounds again at very low volumes. If possible, start with a remote control, so your dog doesn't see it.

As soon as you hear the sounds, feed your dog or start playing with them. Once your dog is done eating or playing, turn off the sounds immediately. This is how they begin to associate the sound with something positive. Do this several times over the course of a few days until your dog starts to get excited when he hears the sounds. Once your dog has made this first connection, you can begin to increase the volume slightly each time.

Finally, your dog will begin to associate sounds with something fun like eating or playing, and it will be much easier to keep them quiet in noisy situations. Once your dog is less receptive and your emotional response to loud sounds has changed, we still recommend taking steps to control your stress in specific situations. For example, fireworks are a common trigger for dogs that are stressed and worried.

If your dog is still stressed by loud noises after trying these steps, you should consult your veterinarian for more advice. If the noise of your dog's phobia is very serious, or if you find that your attempts to desensitize it are not working, or making things worse, I advise you to seek an animal behavior specialist to help you. Your veterinarian or instructor can advise you.

Prevention of noise anxiety in dogs

Many behaviorists and dog trainers believe that puppies go through a period of "fear impression" between eight and twenty weeks when they learn what is safe in the great world and what is not. Exposure to traumatic stimuli during this period can have lasting effects, as can fireworks with Keli. The same exposure outside of this critical period may temporarily scare a dog but is much less likely to cause permanent damage to his psyche. Obviously, therefore, the first step in handling noise phobias is prevention. During this period of "fear impression" of the life of a young puppy, it is essential to take more precautions to ensure that it is not traumatized by unusually loud or sudden noises.

Even later, in a dog's life, it is important to avoid experiences, such as confining the dog near an object that produces noise, which could trigger an unhealthy fear of loud noises.

In fact, there may be a genetic predisposition for the development of fearful behaviors, which would help explain why a dog can tolerate a strong impulse repeated with impunity, while others only need to be exposed to the same stimulus to develop a serious behavior problem. But what do we do with the thousands of phobic dogs for whom prevention is no longer an option? The damage is already done. Are they condemned to live the rest of their lives hidden under the bed every time the storm clouds gather?

It is a serious concern. Animal shelters report universally that July 5 and January 1 are the two busiest days of the year in their kennels, taking care of the dogs that fled the night before. Fear-induced adrenaline causes dogs to climb fences that would normally be more than adequate to keep them confined safely. Some even go through windows and dig doors in their frantic attempts to escape the torment of noise.

Fortunately, there are ways to desensitize dogs with noise phobia. It takes time and real effort on the part of the dog owner to follow a noise desensitization program, but if followed faithfully, have a good chance of success.

CHAPTER TEN
ANTI-ANXIETY DRUGS AND DOGS

Dogs are remarkably complex animals that react to their environment in several ways. Dogs not only experience a wide range of emotions, but they can also suffer from many of the same mental illnesses as their owners. In fact, your dog's stress levels may even synchronize with yours. Anxiety, in particular, is increasing in both dogs and humans. It is estimated that 18% of American adults will suffer from an anxiety disorder at some time. Meanwhile, it is believed that 14% of dogs experience separation anxiety. Some stimuli, such as loud noises and new or unknown environments, can scare dogs and cause a terrifying response. However, fear is not the same as an anxiety disorder. Before buying any medicine to calm dogs, there are some things to consider.

The common forms of anxiety in dogs include generalized anxiety and separation anxiety. Dogs with generalized anxiety may react with fear of stimuli that would not affect the other dogs with such force. Dogs with separation anxiety are stressed when they separate from their owners. This often results in destructive or unwanted behavior, which includes restlessness, dirt, chewing furniture and other properties. A less common form of anxiety is related to old age. Older dogs diagnosed with cognitive dysfunction syndrome are prone to develop anxiety, in addition to other mental disorders, as their brain function decreases.

Do soothing pills really work?

Veterinarians may prescribe medications to treat your dog's anxiety, which will fall largely into the categories of selective serotonin reuptake inhibitors (SSRIs) and sedatives for dogs. Some of the most common anti-anxiety medications you can find include SSRIs, benzodiazapenes and buspirone.

Selective serotonin reuptake inhibitors

SSRIs increase serotonin to relieve anxiety and stress. Some SSRIs, such as fluoxetine and clomipramine, have been approved by the FDA for the treatment of separation anxiety in dogs. SSRIs can take up to a week or up to a month to take effect. They can also cause serotonin toxicity when given together with other anxiety medications, such as trazodone, tricyclic antidepressants and monoamine oxidase inhibitors. The side effects of SSRI medications include agitation, increased anxiety levels, loss of appetite, increased risk of seizures, sedation and tremor.

Benzodiazepines

Benzodiazepine works as sedatives to reassure the dog. This type of medication is usually used as a short-term solution as needed and generally has an immediate effect. Benzodiazepines are particularly effective for the treatment of separation anxiety and can be prescribed in combination with some antidepressants. Side effects include loss of coordination, agitation, overeating and sedation.

Buspirone

Buspirone is a psychotropic drug, which changes the way neurotransmitters communicate in the brain. It is especially effective for dogs with generalized anxiety, although it is best used in dogs with unprecedented aggressive behavior. While buspirone has fewer side effects than some of the other drugs used to calm dogs with anxiety, it can also increase anxiety.

Monoamine oxidase inhibitors

Dogs that suffer from age-related anxiety and cognitive dysfunction syndrome can benefit from a stronger type of antidepressant known as monoamine oxidase inhibitors. Like most antidepressants, this medication increases serotonin levels and is also approved by the FDA for use in dogs. Symptoms include agitation, vomiting, diarrhea and disorientation.

Safety measures

Although behavioral medications formulated for humans, including antidepressants and SSRIs, are commonly used in veterinary practice, many of these medications have not been widely tested or approved in animals. However, there are dosing guidelines to help veterinarians prescribe these medications and they are generally considered safe for veterinary use. Like all medications, anti-anxiety medications for dogs have side effects.

Natural and safer alternatives that can be prescribed or recommended, along with other drugs, to calm dogs. Pheromones, particularly Adaptil, are excellent alternatives to prescription medications. Products that contain pheromones, including collars and diffusers, are available in most pet stores. Dietary adaptations can also help calm dogs with anxiety. Socialization and obedience training can help control and even prevent anxiety in dogs.

Find the best option

Medications can be a good way to combat your dog's anxiety if it is a debilitating part of his daily life. However, it is useful to be aware of the potential dangers and difficulties of using medications to calm dogs, as well as the threat posed by medications that have not been prescribed by a veterinarian, especially over-the-counter sedatives for dogs. Commonly, the veterinarian will attempt to encourage the use of behavioral therapy and slow exposure to stressors to help the dog overcome its problems on its own. Pharmaceutical solutions are usually the last resort. As always, it is advisable to consult a veterinarian before deciding that the anxious dog needs medications.

Side effects of anti-anxiety drugs

Anxiety medications are known in human circles as a means to reduce the levels of stress or anxiety associated with those stress levels.

These types of drugs are being investigated more frequently these days for some of the same behaviors in dogs. While some work quite well in certain animals, some do not and others still, others can be dangerous or even fatal to their beloved member of the dog family. Side effects are simply adverse reactions to a substance. Anxiety medications are defined as medications administered to calm, relax and modify anxiety in dogs.

Symptoms of side effects of the anxiety medicines in dogs

Anxiety in your dog can be shown in different ways or behaviors. Some of the side effects of anxiety medications may include:

- Lethargy
- Irregularities of heart rate
- Increased levels of anxiety/stress.
- Intestinal and urinary changes (increase or decrease in frequency, changes in consistency, etc.)
- Vomits
- Reduced muscle control
- Lower blood pressure
- Weakness

Types of side effects of anxiety medications

The types of side effects are found in their type of medical medication that refers to how they control anxiety problems:

H1 antagonists

- These are medications like Benadryl that work well for allergies and work well to calm your puppy

- Side effects include drowsiness, fatigue, urinary retention, late reaction and dry mouth.

Benzodiazepines

- These drugs have a potentiating effect on some neurotransmitters

- Side effects include loss of coordination, drowsiness, changes in appetite and sedation.

SSRI

- These medications have an effect on the reabsorption of serotonin (fluoxetine or Paxil)

- Side effects include vomiting, diarrhea, fatigue and gasping.

Causes of side effects

The causes of side effects of anxiety medications in dogs come from several sources:

- Pre-existing conditions or pathologies not diagnosed or underlying

- Dosage deviations or incorrect calculations of the required dose.

- Diagnosis of heart, liver or lung diseases that react with the anxiety given.

- Serotonin syndrome: This is a specific condition that occurs when a medication is used that causes the accumulation of natural levels of serotonin in the host's body.

The causes of anxiety in your beloved pet also come from several sources:

- Separation anxiety: this is the most common trigger in most domestic dogs

- Social anxiety

- Noise anxiety

Diagnosis of the secondary effects of the anxiety of medicines in dogs

When your veterinarian becomes involved in the process of diagnosing the anxious behaviors of your family pet, you will need some valuable advice from him. Your complete history, in this case, will not only require the inclusion of the patient's usual eating habits and activity levels, but also the behaviors he observes in his partner. You will need to know the frequency of each of the symptoms/behaviors you have noticed and the duration of each symptom/behavior. You will probably also want some correlation with specific circumstances that seem to trigger behaviors such as thunderstorms, loud noises, being left alone and strangers entering the house.

Your veterinarian will perform a physical exam and you will probably need to take blood samples for laboratory evaluation. He will try to see if the normal values of blood chemistry are out of line in any area, suggesting that something could change the way the various systems of the canine body do their job. Serotonin and cortisol are two areas of interest in the interpretation of these tests. Serotonin levels cannot actually be measured, such as red and white blood cell counts, for example, but can be evaluated based on other clinical outcomes, verifying the function of the systems affected by serotonin, health history, the behaviors and drugs used in addition to excluding other possibilities.

Treatment of the side effects

The treatment of side effects of anxiety medications in dogs can be multilevel, depending on the side effects and the cause of the anxiety, and can be used alone or in any combination:

- Dose adjustments: some medications work better in some dogs than in others and dose changes may be needed to find the best amount to use, especially since the medication's tolerance and effectiveness may change over time.

- Try other medications as alternatives or in combination with anxiety medications that cause side effects, especially since the side effects may apply to cardiac arrhythmias or liver problems.

- Behavioral training or retraining of the dog or dog's family: this may include things like changing the time of your care activities, such as petting, grooming and playing with your puppy so that he is ready for a nap when he has to leave him alone, or make him take a long walk before leaving (helping you be ready to rest again) or offer your favorite toy just before leaving

These changes in activity can reduce the sudden departure and anxiety and fear of separation experienced by the member of your dog. Complete cessation of synthetic anxiety medications instead of more natural remedies. Other behavioral techniques that can ultimately help in a more natural and safe way to manage anxiety behaviors.

__Recovery of the side effects__

For some dogs, changes in pet behavior, as well as favorite family members, can help relieve the anxiety behaviors exhibited by your pet. But, for those dogs in which these various changes in behavior fail to control anxiety in your pet, medications may be the answer. It is not a good idea to venture only on the drug route. It is necessary to use the experience and training of a reliable veterinary professional for the guidance and administration of these medications.

Just as one does not venture on this path only for a member of the human family without the help and direction of the family doctor, one should not do the same for the beloved member of the canine family.

Your veterinarian can work with you to find the right regimen to control anxiety behaviors in your pet to avoid the side effects of anxiety medications in dogs.

CHAPTER ELEVEN
NATURAL REMEDIES
FOR ANXIOUS DOGS

There are many ways to help an anxious dog and these natural solutions are an excellent starting point. Anxiety is very common among dogs for a wide range of reasons, sometimes situational and sometimes based on personality. Anxiety manifests itself through different fears or phobias and is expressed through various behaviors, which include constant barking, licking or excessive healing, destroying anything, from clothing to walls and door frames, to eliminate the interior even when it breaks or even react aggressively to people or other animals.

Many anxieties and phobias can be relieved by training and conditioning. For example, separation anxiety is extremely common among dogs and can often be significantly improved or even eliminated by the gradual conditioning of being alone with positive reinforcement.

Nevertheless, some dogs are simply anxious in their general disposition or need help to calm down enough before training them to overcome a stressful situation. For these dogs, there are some natural solutions that you can try. Even dogs still need training; there is no magic cure to correct fear and anxiety forever. But the natural solutions listed below can be of great help to help a dog cope when the real solutions (long-term training, desensitization and conditioning) take hold.

When considering your dog's treatment for anxiety, it is important to know the source of the anxiety. Is your dog eager to be alone? Be confined? Is anxiety caused by loud noises, travel or sudden changes in the environment or routine? Some dogs have phobias of specific objects, types of people or specific situations. The source reports the treatment considerably. For example, relaxing music can help a dog with separation anxiety, but it will not help a dog that is eager to walk in crowded places. There are pharmaceutical products available for veterinarians for extreme cases, but to minimize dog care and the appearance of possible side effects, try these options before requesting a prescription.

Exercise

Exercising can be one of the most crucial components to help an anxious dog. Like exercise, it is an excellent anti-stress for men, as well as for dogs.

Exercise accomplishes some things when it helps a dog deal with anxiety. First, it spurs the production of serotonin, that pleasant chemical that we humans also receive when we train or walk. Second, it eliminates repressed energy and tension that can exacerbate anxiety. Burn all the doggy style of extra energy every day through a long recovery game, a walk, running by your side while riding a bike or other favorite activities can do a lot to reduce problems with problems such as separation anxiety or nervous tension. Just as the saying, a good dog is a tired dog.

Distraction

If your dog is nervous about certain situations, such as fireworks or thunderstorms, or is even nervous about being in a crowd, distraction can work wonders.

Engaging your dog's brain at work will help you focus on you and the things you know, instead of the unknown around you that scares you.

Even if it is not the time to start a new training, it is a good time to practice the tricks that your dog knows and for which you can earn rewards. Try to reward your dog with treats for simple commands such as sitting, standing, lying down, shaking, sitting, rolling and other tricks he likes. Another possibility, particularly for dogs that are very motivated by food, is to distract your dog with puzzle games such as a trick or a jug ball, or even a frozen Kong toy stuffed with peanut butter. This can also help you associate scary things like loud or strange noises that come with much-appreciated rewards so that the event goes from being scary to be at least tolerable.

Thundershirt

Thundershirt is a common solution for dog anxiety. It is a tight garment that surrounds your dog.

The idea is that the sensation of continuous pressure can help calm a dog's nerves for things like travel anxiety and, as the name implies, noise anxiety, among other problems.

However, there is no definitive scientific evidence to prove that they really work. Some dog owners swear it; Others found that it didn't help. The effectiveness of Thundershirt can also depend on when and how it is used, as well as the personality and particular needs of the dog in which it is used. So, something like this could be useful when used in conjunction with other natural solutions, since each one helps to improve the benefits of the other.

Relaxing massage

Massage is an excellent way to calm the brain of an anxious dog. And yes, you don't need a massage table this. Everyone loves a nice massage and the same can be said about our pets. Massage can help calm an anxious dog using long, slow movements to calm the nerves. A popular method of dog massage is called TTouch.

It is "a process based on circular movements of the fingers and hands over the whole body. The intention of the TTouch is to activate cellular function and awaken cellular intelligence."

The result is a relaxed dog. Besides, studies have shown that petting a dog can also help calm the nerves, making it a beneficial solution for everyone.

Pheromone for dogs

Scents can also help calm an anxious dog and DAP is a popular option. It is a synthesized chemical that is based on a hormone produced by lactating females that helps keep their puppies calm and increases their bond with it. While scientific studies have shown that DAP works with puppies, it is not so clear if it works with anxious adult dogs. Even so, there is a possibility that you can help, and it can be one of the many tools used to help an anxious dog. It looks like a plug-in speaker with vials that last about thirty days and humans can't smell it.

Relaxing music

Music can really have a calming effect on anxious dogs. Humans are not the only species that can calm down with soothing music. Many owners leave the television or radio on when they leave the house to help a dog feel comfortable. But there is also specialized music that you can play to help certain anxious dogs. The underlying psychoacoustic theory that informs through a dog's ear is summed up in just two words: simple sound. This refers to the process of minimizing the intricate auditory information found in most music. The dog's ear is intentionally selected, organized and recorded to provide easy auditory assimilation. Music can help in a variety of situations, such as separation anxiety and travel anxiety. There are also compilations designed to help desensitize a dog with noise phobias.

Rescue remedy and supplements

Even if I look for natural solutions that you can make yourself or collect at the pet store, I recommend that you consult your veterinarian before trying supplements, even natural ones.

That said, Rescue Remedy is a popular solution for those who rely on herbal supplements to treat anxiety. Rescue Remedy is a mixture of natural extracts of herbs and flowers that can calm the nerves. It comes in everything from drops to sprays and gums for humans, and they really have a specific pet mix. You can add a few drops to your dog's water dish or add a drop to a treat. Another possible supplement is the Animal Essentials Tranquility Mix formula.

CHAPTER TWELVE
TEN RELAXING TIPS FOR ANXIOUS DOGS

Tip #1: Confirm anxiety

To help an anxious dog, you must first be absolutely certain that it is really anxious, and that any unusual behavior does not manifest itself due to a medical problem such as a neurological or thyroid disease. Although a trip to the vet can cause stress on its own, it is very important to rule out medical conditions because some anxiety symptoms can be very similar to those shown by a dog that does not feel well. These may include vocalizing more than usual, hiding, shaking and showing reluctance to enjoy normal behaviors such as playing.

Excessive care/licking and improper urination may be signs of anxiety, but they may also be symptomatic of other conditions such as allergic skin diseases (excessive care) and urinary tract disorders (inappropriate urination). Once the veterinarian has diagnosed anxiety, referral to a qualified canine behaviorist may be recommended. This can be very helpful, especially if you are not sure what causes your dog's acute stress.

Tip #2. Establish the root cause

Look at all the possible reasons why your dog might feel anxious. Keeping a diary can be useful. Has there been any change in your daily routine? Sometimes it can be easy to determine why a dog is stressed; for example, the arrival of a new pet or a new baby. Other times it can be difficult because stressful events can go unnoticed; for example, something that happens or is happening when your dog stays home without you. Separation anxiety is the most common anxiety that affects companion dogs.

Sometimes, a single event that has scared the dog can become a persistent and excessive fear known as a phobia. It is possible that related events may act as triggers. For example, similar noises may sound like a stimulus to a dog that is phobic from thunderstorms. Associated events or anything that brings back a memory of the storm can also cause anxiety even if there is no storm. The most common phobias that affect dogs are related to noise.

Tip #3. Nutrition and behavior

Diet can influence canine behavior. Dogs digest, metabolize and use different diets with varying degrees of efficiency and, sometimes, a product with alternative ingredients and/or a different nutritional balance (the way in which proteins, fats and carbohydrates are balanced) will alter the sugar in the blood. Serotonin levels and speed at which energy is released. If your dog was behaving normally with its original food, try changing it to see if its behavior returns to normal.

Irregular food intake can also cause blood sugar fluctuations, so make sure your dog eats enough and on a regular schedule. Anxious dogs may not eat and this may increase symptoms due to the drop in serotonin levels. Some dyes and chemical preservatives have been shown to contribute to learning difficulties and hyperactivity in humans. Like very sensitive children who react poorly to some additives, dogs can suffer some adverse reactions (although this is largely based on anecdotal rather than scientific evidence).

Tip #4. Pheromone therapy

Pheromone therapy is another effective way to help calm an anxious dog, although it should be emphasized that this does not deny the need to try to establish the root cause of the problem and eliminate or minimize, where possible, stressful events. Pheromone products contain adapotyl, which is a synthetic copy of the natural comforting pheromone that releases a prey to reassure its puppies. You can choose between Adaptil spray (for use in bedding), necklaces and diffusers.

Tip #5. Behavior modification

It is very important to take active measures to help the dog relax. Remember that each dog is different, the causes of anxiety can be very variable and the most effective methods to help calm the dog will vary depending on the individual. Some dogs, for instance, feel very safe in a cage, while others may panic if childbirth is forced. In general, it is not advisable to reassure the dog in panic, as this can strengthen and reward behavior. It is better to try to avoid fear and calm the dog in the best possible way before the event. Never punish anxious behavior. This can make things worse.

Desensitization and counterconditioning are more effective in dogs that recently began to suffer anxiety. The desensitizer describes the dog's repeated exposure to the stimulus that causes fear, but at a level so low that it cannot cause a nervous response.

Counterconditioning describes the dog's training to perform positive behavior instead of negative behavior; for example, sit and stay instead of disappearing. Desensitizing CDs are available for dogs that fear fireworks and other noises. These are sound-based treatment programs that use specially recorded sounds along with simple training methods.

Tip #6. Separation anxiety

As mentioned, separation anxiety is common in dogs and is the most common specific anxiety that affects them. Be sure to spend adequate quality time with your dog. This means reserving special time for grooming and play, but not focusing your attention on the dog while at home, as this can aggravate the problem. If possible, it may be helpful to leave the dog for short periods; and before leaving home or returning home, ignore it. Make sure that the environment in which it is left is adequate, with safe toys (such as a padded Kong to keep it occupied) and a comfortable bed.

Some dogs like to look outside through a window (although others may get nervous or excited by passersby). Some may feel more relaxed if a radio is left on for quiet background noise. The help of a behaviorist may be necessary if the dog suffers from separation anxiety and medications can help in combination with behavioral therapy. A well-socialized puppy is less likely to suffer from this condition. In a dog that already suffers from separation anxiety, it may be helpful to help him become less dependent or fixed or a person (if he has a favorite family member), so if there is another person who can perform feeding and care tasks A Sometimes, this can strengthen ties between the dog and other family members and help increase their trust with them and decrease their dependence on you.

Tip #7. Medications

DOG anxiety is serious because it is an unpleasant condition for both the dog and the owner. In cases where a dog suffers prolonged periods of stress or is demonstrating problematic behaviors such as aggression or inappropriate urination; Veterinary prescription medications can be very useful. Medications should be used only under the guidance of the veterinarian and may not be suitable for dogs with liver or kidney dysfunction. Some medications (e.g., benzodiazepines) are only suitable for short-term use, as they can affect memory and cause lethargy.

Benzodiazepines reduce the dog's response to fear and have an immediate calming effect. Azapirones can be used to treat phobias and fear aggression. They are not useful for panic disorders, but they can be effective in case of more generalized anxiety. Tricyclic antidepressants (ATC) can be used for anxiety, panic, phobias and compulsive behaviors, such as chasing shadows or licking excessively. Sometimes they are used to treat aggressive help behaviors caused by underlying anxiety. Selective serotonin reuptake inhibitors (SSRIs) act longer and are considered safer than TCA. They affect the dog's serotonin production and can be useful for compulsive behavior and aggression. Medications should be used in combination with, not in place of behavioral therapy.

Tip #8. Natural remedies

There are several natural remedies available that can help calm anxious dogs.

These include Adaptil tablets, which contain a combination of vitamins GABA, L-tryptophan, L-theanine and B and are a pheromone-free calming tool that can be used to help dogs during stressful events. Another option is Kalm Aid, which contains L-tryptophan and L-theanine. L-tryptophan is a precursor to serotonin (the happy hormone), while L-theanine stimulates the release of dopamine, a neurotransmitter responsible for confidence and the feeling of well-being. The effectiveness of floral remedies is questionable, but Bach Rescue Remedy Pet is a safe and alcohol-free option for dogs. Thundershirts are not a remedy as such but fall under the umbrella of the "natural cure." These work by exerting light and constant pressure on the dog's torso and many owners report that this has a calming effect.

Tip #9. Minimizes stress

Many dogs may be perfectly happy most of the time, but they may not cope with certain stressful situations that occur irregularly.

Examples may include fireworks phobia, fear of storms, travel or visiting the veterinarian. Needless to say, it is essential to keep your dog safe inside when there are fireworks or storms. Behavioral changes and/or medications may be necessary if the dog becomes very stressed. Desensitization is effective for many dogs, but it must be started early to be effective.

Tip #10. Keep calm

Try to stay calm. Dogs are very sensitive creatures and soon learn how their humans feel. Try to ignore all unacceptable behavior as much as possible, because attention itself is a reward. Try to avoid your dog's behavior and distract him before he can participate in an undesirable one. This can really help because the familiarity of a certain routine can reinforce certain behaviors. Doing something different (for example, instigating a new game or asking him to do something for you like "sitting" or "going to bed") instead of just anticipating the behavior can be helpful.

Punishing the dog will not work and could make things worse because this increases the unpredictability of the environment and can increase fear, which in turn can damage your dog's confidence in you and cause or worsen aggression.

CHAPTER THIRTEEN EXTRA WAYS TO KEEP YOUR DOG HAPPY AND HEALTHY

These are all excellent ways to prevent your dog from falling into patterns of fear and anxiety. But there are also many other things you can do! Here are some additional tips to calm your dog:

- Go for a walk: walks are essential ways for your dog to exercise and are also good for your dog's mental health. They help you experiment with new things, see new places, escape the extra energy and leave the house.

- Train your dog: dogs like to make their owners happy. So, by training your dog, you help him know how to please you. This makes them both a little happier and simplifies life.

- Teach your dog a new trick: this not only provides your dog with mental stimulation, but it is also an excellent way for you two to spend time together.

- Get more playtime: spend more time before and after work playing with your dog. This helps you consume more energy and allows you to spend more time with you, which will always lead you to a healthier and happier puppy.

- Establish consistency: if there are no clear patterns in your family, your dog will be confused. One day, certain behaviors win a surprise, but other days earn a difficult word. Sometimes you don't go for days at a time and sometimes you don't. By establishing clear and consistent patterns, this gives your dog more peace of mind.

- Praise your dog: dogs love feeling as if they make him happy. By giving them compliments, affection and goodies, you are helping to ensure their happiness and tranquility.

- Calm an anxious dog with supplements: Some dogs do not simply respond to training. In cases like this, veterinarians may prescribe anti-anxiety medications or other medications to help the dog calm down. If you prefer not to give your dog such medications, the solution may be calming supplements. Calming supplements such as anti-stress protection formulas provide vitamins, minerals and food supplements that support the nervous system and a calm dog.

With time, patience, training, exercise and perhaps relaxing supplements, you can calm your anxious dog and enjoy the special bond they share together.

A healthy and happy dog

We all want our dogs to lead a life as happy and healthy as possible. It can be difficult for them to do this when their life is governed by anxiety. Breaking these cycles and establishing new habits is not an easy task. It takes patience, dedication and willingness to give your dog the best of your attention and time. But with time, patience, training and exercise, you can calm your anxious dog and enjoy the special bond they share together.

CONCLUSION

The key to helping your dog calm down is to keep calm and show your dog that he has nothing to worry about. Dogs are very sensitive and if you get stiff and start worrying about how you will face a dog in panic, your dog will take over and make them feel even more anxious. Be as real as possible about your anxiety. Do not make a fuss or try to comfort them excessively because, again, you will transform it into something bigger than it is. Keep calm around you.

It is believed that anxious dogs often assumed the role of the leader of the pack, making them responsible for the safety of the rest of the pack. This is a very stressful position for a dog that lives in a human world since they often do not understand it and will see all kinds of things as a potential threat to the pack (like the mailman) that we automatically know is safe.

Therefore, an anxious dog will benefit from the fact that it is clear to you that you are the leader of the pack because the members of the pack take command of Alpha, which means that if the leader is not worried about something it doesn't even have to be. It may take some time for your dog to change his mind about his place in the pack, but once he has done so, his anxiety will decrease as he learns to trust you.

The dog's anxiety is unlikely to disappear if ignored since the dog's behavioral problems caused by his anxiety are more likely to get worse over time. Therefore, as an owner, you must invest time and patience to understand your dog's anxiety and use the training and products available consistently to make the necessary changes to create a calm and happy dog. Your dog is a precious part of your life. When you are not happy and suffer from anxiety, it is not only difficult for your pet, but also for you. You want your friend to be happy, be happy and feel safe, and when that is not the case, it also causes anxiety.

With these anxiety solutions, your dog's anxiety will be a thing of the past and your dog will be able to leave behind those feelings of insecurity and insecurity, thus enjoying you and live in a more complete and satisfying way.

AUTHOR NOTE

First of all, thank you for purchasing this Book.

If you enjoyed this book and found some benefits in reading it, I'd be extremely delighted to hear from you and hope that you could take some time to post a review on Amazon. Your feedback and support will help me as an Author to greatly improve my writing craft for future projects and make this book even better.

I want you to know that your review is very important and so if you'd like to leave a review, all you have to do is to submit it through your Amazon Account.

I wish you all the best in your future endeavors!

Printed in Great Britain
by Amazon